contents

NZ, Canada, US and UK readers
Please note that Australian cup and spoon
measurements are metric. A conversion
chart appears on page 62.

party time!

Put a little effort into organising your party now so that, on the day, the festivities run seamlessly

get organised

Being organised saves you money and prevents you from becoming stressed. Accomplish all you can in the lead-up to your party; make a list of what can be done each day of the week before the event. Most of our recipes tell you how far in advance they can be made – this will help you plan your time. With a little forethought, you will find yourself happily mingling with your friends on the night, confident that everything's going to plan.

choice of food

It's a good idea to serve a mixture of cold and hot savouries. But know your limitations: it is better to choose a few dishes that go well together than to be over-ambitious and make too many.

Choose your selection of finger food in light of the nature of the occasion, the season, time of day, duration of the event and the number of people in attendance. When choosing the recipes, think about complementary colours, textures and flavours. The time of year determines what people like to eat – and what produce is available – so the month you choose will also act as a guide to the kind of menu you should create. Serve light dishes in summer and more robust bites in winter. Remember to check on the food requirements of your guests beforehand – vegetarian, kosher, low-fat, etc.

how much food?

Making sure you provide the right amount of food is paramount to the success of your party. Below is some advice to help you decide how much food you should make.

For pre-dinner nibbles: allow four to five pieces of food per person.

For a cocktail party: allow four to five pieces of food per person for the first hour, then four pieces of food per person for each hour after that.

For a full afternoon or evening: allow 12 to 14 pieces of food per person for the duration of the whole party.

drinks

Drinks quantities can be hard to estimate. There is a general rule that 10 guests will consume 20 drinks on average at a cocktail party. If it's a full-evening affair, though, this increases to 40 drinks. One budget-conscious tip is to offer a selection of cocktails made from one or two primary spirits only, or just limit the choice to wine and beer. Regardless of the time of year, you can never have too much ice. There is nothing worse than serving warm drinks. If you have limited space in your fridge or freezer, a good idea is to store the ice and drinks in your dishwasher. Place the cans and bottles in the racks and cover them with ice; you can chill your glasses there, too. The drinks are out of harm's way, are insulated and will remain cold, and the melted ice drains out below – too easy!

A laundry tub or a child's wading pool are other good places to keep your drinks chilled with ice. Make sure you have a bag or two of "clean" ice to add to drinks.

shortcuts

Here are a few suggestions if you're pressed for time:

- Remember that you can prepare some food a few weeks in advance and freeze it.
- There are a multitude of prepared foods at your local supermarket. Use bottled antipasto ingredients or cheeses and arrange a platter in minutes. Present purchased dips in attractive serving bowls with a selection of crackers and chips for dipping.
- Cold meats and seafood are also easily arranged on large platters, and look fantastic with very little effort.
- Use bottled ingredients, such as pesto or tapenade, instead of making your own.
- Buy prepared sushi from your local Japanese takeaway, but be sure to do so at the last minute to ensure it is absolutely fresh.

checklist

Here is a brief list of equipment you may need to throw a party. If you don't have enough of one thing or another, try to borrow it from a friend, or phone a party hire company.

Cutlery
Plates
Glasses or plastic cups
Serving trays and platters
Serving bowls
Tea and coffee equipment
Oven trays
Airtight storage containers
Fridge and freezer space
Hot plates
Small tables
Napkins
Decorations
Music
Garbage bins
Coasters
Chairs
Marquee (if outdoors)
Fans or heaters

salt and pepper skewered prawns

18 uncooked king prawns (1kg)
2 teaspoons sea salt
¼ teaspoon chinese five-spice powder
½ teaspoon freshly ground black pepper

Peel and devein prawns leaving tails intact.
Thread each prawn onto a skewer lengthways.
Combine remaining ingredients in small bowl.
Cook skewers on heated oiled barbecue
(or grill pan or pan-fry) over high heat until
browned on both sides and just cooked
through, sprinkle with half of the salt mixture
during cooking.
Serve prawn skewers sprinkled with
remaining salt mixture.

makes 18
per skewer 0.2g fat; 103kJ (25 cal)
do ahead Prawns can be peeled and
skewered up to six hours ahead. Cook
skewers just before serving.

spring rolls

20g rice vermicelli
2 teaspoons peanut oil
100g pork mince
1 clove garlic, crushed
1 small fresh red thai chilli,
    chopped finely
1 green onion,
    chopped finely
1 small carrot (70g),
    grated finely
1 teaspoon finely chopped
    coriander root and stems
1 teaspoon fish sauce
50g shelled cooked prawns,
    chopped finely
1 teaspoon cornflour
2 teaspoons water
12 x 12cm-square
    spring roll wrappers
vegetable oil, for deep-frying
cucumber dipping sauce
½ lebanese cucumber (60g),
    seeded, sliced thinly
¼ cup (55g) sugar
½ cup (125ml) water
¼ cup (60ml) white vinegar
2cm piece fresh
    ginger (10g), grated
½ teaspoon salt
1 small fresh red thai chilli,
    sliced thinly
1 green onion, sliced thinly
2 teaspoons chopped
    fresh coriander

Place vermicelli in medium heatproof bowl; cover with boiling water. Stand until just tender; drain. Using kitchen scissors, cut vermicelli into random lengths.

Heat oil in wok or large frying pan; stir-fry pork, garlic and chilli until pork is changed in colour. Add onion, carrot, coriander root and stem, fish sauce and prawns; stir-fry until vegetables just soften. Place stir-fried mixture in small bowl with vermicelli; cool.

Meanwhile, make cucumber dipping sauce.

Blend cornflour with the water in small bowl. Place 1 level tablespoon of the filling near one corner of each wrapper. Lightly brush edges of each wrapper with cornflour mixture; roll to enclose filling, folding in ends.

Just before serving, heat oil in wok or large saucepan; deep-fry spring rolls, in batches, until golden brown. Drain on absorbent paper; serve with cucumber dipping sauce.

Cucumber dipping sauce Place cucumber in heatproof serving bowl. Combine sugar, the water, vinegar, ginger and salt in small saucepan, stir over heat without boiling until sugar is dissolved; pour over cucumber. Sprinkle with chilli, onion and coriander; refrigerate, covered, until chilled.

makes 12

per spring roll 3.5g fat; 319kJ (76 cal)
do ahead The spring rolls can be prepared and the cucumber dipping sauce made a day ahead; store them separately, covered, in the refrigerator. Cook spring rolls just before serving.

fish cakes

500g redfish fillets,
  skinned, boned
2 tablespoons thai red
  curry paste
2 fresh kaffir lime
  leaves, torn
2 green onions,
  chopped coarsely
1 tablespoon fish sauce
1 tablespoon lime juice
2 tablespoons finely
  chopped fresh coriander
3 snake beans (30g),
  chopped finely
2 small fresh red thai chillies,
  chopped finely
peanut oil, for deep-frying
sweet chilli dipping sauce
½ cup (125ml) water
¼ cup (60ml) white vinegar
1 teaspoon hoisin sauce
1 small fresh red thai chilli,
  chopped finely
½ cup (100g) firmly packed
  brown sugar

Cut fish into small pieces. Blend or process fish with curry paste, lime leaves, onion, sauce and juice until mixture forms a smooth paste. Combine fish mixture in medium bowl with coriander, beans and chilli.

Divide mixture into 16 portions; roll each portion into a ball, then flatten into a cake shape.

Make sweet chilli dipping sauce.

Just before serving, heat oil in wok or large saucepan; deep-fry fish cakes, in batches, until browned and cooked through. Drain on absorbent paper; serve fish cakes with sweet chilli dipping sauce.

Sweet chilli dipping sauce Combine ingredients in small saucepan; stir over heat until sugar is dissolved. Bring to a boil; simmer, uncovered, about 5 minutes or until thickened slightly.

makes 16
per fish cake 5.2g fat; 410kJ (97 cal)
do ahead The fish cakes can be prepared and the sweet chilli dipping sauce made a day ahead; store them separately, covered, in the refrigerator. Cook the fish cakes just before serving.

money bags

1 tablespoon peanut oil

1 small brown onion (80g),
   chopped finely

1 clove garlic, crushed

4cm piece fresh ginger
   (20g), grated

100g chicken mince

1 tablespoon finely grated
   palm sugar

1 tablespoon finely chopped
   roasted unsalted peanuts

2 teaspoons finely chopped
   fresh coriander

3 green onions

24 x 8cm-square
   wonton wrappers

vegetable oil, for
   deep-frying

peanut dipping sauce

2 teaspoons peanut oil

1 clove garlic, crushed

½ small brown onion (40g),
   chopped finely

1 small fresh red thai chilli,
   seeded, chopped coarsely

½ stick fresh lemon grass,
   chopped finely

⅓ cup (80ml) coconut milk

1 tablespoon fish sauce

1 tablespoon brown sugar

¼ cup (70g) crunchy
   peanut butter

¼ teaspoon curry powder

2 teaspoons lime juice

Heat oil in wok or large frying pan; stir-fry onion, garlic and ginger until onion softens. Add chicken; stir-fry until chicken is changed in colour. Add sugar; stir-fry about 3 minutes or until sugar dissolves. Stir in nuts and coriander; cool.

Meanwhile, cut upper green half of each onion into four long slices; reserve remaining onion half for another use. Submerge onion strips in hot water for a few seconds to make pliable.

Place 12 wrappers on board; cover each wrapper with another, placed on the diagonal to form star shape.

Place rounded teaspoons of chicken mixture in centre of each star; gather corners to form pouch shape. Tie green onion slice around neck of each pouch to hold closed, secure with toothpick.

Make peanut dipping sauce.

Just before serving, heat oil in wok or large saucepan; deep-fry money bags, in batches, until crisp and browned lightly. Drain on absorbent paper; remove toothpicks then serve with peanut dipping sauce.

Peanut dipping sauce Heat oil in small saucepan; cook garlic and onion until softened. Stir in remaining ingredients; bring to a boil. Reduce heat; simmer, stirring, until sauce thickens slightly.

makes 12

per money bag 10.2g fat; 681kJ (162 cal)

do ahead Uncooked money bags are suitable to freeze; use a sheet of baking paper between each layer of money bags. There's no need to defrost them before cooking. The peanut dipping sauce can be made a day ahead; store, covered, in the refrigerator.

mussels with garlic crumbs

1 cup (70g) stale breadcrumbs
2 cloves garlic, chopped finely
1 teaspoon finely grated lemon rind
2 tablespoons finely chopped fresh flat-leaf parsley
60 small black mussels (1kg)
1½ cups (375ml) water
¼ cup (60ml) extra virgin olive oil

Combine breadcrumbs, garlic, rind and parsley in small bowl; mix well.

Wash and scrub mussels, remove fibrous beards by pulling firmly.

Bring the water to a boil in large saucepan; add mussels and boil, covered, until mussels open, shaking pan occasionally. Discard any mussels that do not open.

Break open shells, discard tops. Loosen mussels from shells with a spoon, return to shells. Place shells in single layer on large baking tray.

Sprinkle mussels with breadcrumb mixture, then drizzle with oil. Place under hot grill about 1 minute or until browned.

makes 60
per mussel 2g fat; 126kJ (30 cal)
do ahead Mussels can be prepared with breadcrumb topping several hours ahead. Grill just before serving.

goat cheese and potato fritters

600g potatoes, chopped
¼ cup (60ml) cream
¼ teaspoon ground nutmeg
3 eggs, beaten lightly
2 egg yolks, beaten lightly
½ cup (75g) plain flour
250g firm goat cheese, crumbled
2 tablespoons chopped fresh flat-leaf parsley
pinch cayenne pepper
vegetable oil, for deep-frying

Boil, steam or microwave potato until tender; drain. Mash potato in large bowl with cream and nutmeg until smooth. Add egg and egg yolk; using wooden spoon, beat until smooth. Stir in flour, cheese, parsley and pepper.

Heat oil in wok or large saucepan; deep-fry level tablespoons of potato mixture, in batches, until fritters are browned lightly. Drain on absorbent paper.

makes 32
per fritter 4.8g fat; 288kJ (69 cal)
do ahead These fritters are best cooked just before serving.

arancini balls

2½ cups (625ml)
  chicken stock
1 tablespoon olive oil
1 small brown onion (80g),
  chopped finely
1 clove garlic, crushed
½ cup (200g) arborio rice
½ cup (125ml) dry
  white wine
½ cup (60g) frozen peas
40g ham, chopped finely
½ cup (40g) finely grated
  parmesan cheese
60g mozzarella cheese
1 egg, beaten lightly
plain flour
1 egg, beaten lightly, extra
1 tablespoon milk
1 cup (100g) packaged
  dry breadcrumbs
vegetable oil, for deep-frying

Bring stock to a boil in medium saucepan. Reduce heat to low and keep hot.

Heat olive oil in medium saucepan, add onion and garlic; cook, stirring, until onion is soft but not coloured. Add rice; cook, stirring, 2 minutes. Add white wine; cook, stirring, until liquid has evaporated.

Add about ⅓ cup (80ml) of the hot stock; cook, stirring, over low heat until the liquid is absorbed. Repeat until all the stock has been used. Total cooking time will be about 25 minutes.

Stir in peas and ham; remove from heat, stir in parmesan cheese. Transfer risotto to medium heatproof bowl; cool.

Chop mozzarella into 16 pieces.

Stir egg into risotto. Roll 2-level-tablespoon portions of risotto mixture into balls; press a piece of mozzarella into centre of each ball, roll to enclose. Toss balls in flour, shake away excess flour. Dip into combined extra egg and milk, then coat in breadcrumbs.

Heat vegetable oil in deep saucepan; deep-fry arancini, in batches, until browned and heated through. Drain on absorbent paper.

makes 16
per arancini 8.7g fat; 664kJ (158 cal)
do ahead The risotto mixture can be made a day ahead. Arancini can be fried several hours ahead of serving and reheated in a slow oven.

spicy potato pakoras with coriander raita

Besan, a flour made from ground dried chickpeas, is a staple of the Indian kitchen. Pakoras are small Indian fritters that can contain vegetables, meat, fish or rice.

400g potatoes, cut into
   1cm cubes
1 small kumara (250g),
   cut into 1cm cubes
1½ cups (225g) besan
½ teaspoon bicarbonate
   of soda
¾ cup (180ml) water
2 teaspoons peanut oil
2 cloves garlic, crushed
½ teaspoon ground turmeric
1 teaspoon ground cumin
½ teaspoon dried
   chilli flakes
2 green onions,
   chopped finely
vegetable oil, for deep-frying
coriander raita
1 cup (280g) greek-style
   yogurt
½ cup coarsely chopped
   fresh coriander
1 teaspoon ground cumin

Boil, steam or microwave potato and kumara, together, until just tender; drain. Cool 10 minutes. Meanwhile, make coriander raita.

Sift besan and soda into large bowl; gradually add the water, stirring, until batter is smooth.

Heat peanut oil in small frying pan; cook garlic, spices and chilli flakes, stirring, until fragrant. Combine garlic mixture in bowl with batter; stir in potato, kumara and onion.

Heat vegetable oil in wok or large saucepan; deep-fry tablespoons of the mixture, in batches, until pakoras are browned lightly. Drain on absorbent paper; serve with coriander raita.

Coriander raita Combine ingredients in small bowl. Cover; refrigerate 30 minutes.

makes 24 pakoras and 1 cup coriander raita
per pakora 3.4g fat; 302kJ (72 cal)
per tablespoon raita 1.4g fat; 100kJ (24 cal)
do ahead The raita can be made a day ahead; store, covered, in the refrigerator. Pakora are best cooked just before serving.

cheese fillo triangles

150g fetta cheese, crumbled
125g ricotta cheese
1 egg, beaten lightly
pinch ground nutmeg
freshly ground pepper
12 sheets fillo pastry
100g butter, melted

Preheat oven to moderately hot.
Combine fetta, ricotta, egg, nutmeg and pepper
in small bowl; mix well.
To prevent pastry from drying out, cover with plastic
wrap, then a damp tea towel while making triangles.
Layer two sheets of pastry, brushing both sheets
with a little butter.
Cut layered sheets into four strips lengthways.
Place two teaspoons of cheese mixture at one
end of each pastry strip. Fold one corner end of
pastry diagonally across filling to other edge to
form a triangle. Continue folding to end of strip,
retaining triangle shape.
Brush triangles with a little butter. Repeat with
remaining pastry, filling and butter.
Place triangles on greased oven trays;
bake in moderately hot oven about 15 minutes
or until browned.

makes 24
per triangle 5.8g fat; 328kJ (78 cal)
do ahead The uncooked triangles are suitable to
freeze; use a sheet of baking paper between each
layer of triangles. There's no need to defrost them
before cooking.

curry puffs

2 teaspoons peanut oil
2 teaspoons finely chopped
   coriander root
2 green onions,
   chopped finely
1 clove garlic, crushed
100g beef mince
½ teaspoon ground turmeric
½ teaspoon ground cumin
¼ teaspoon ground
   coriander
2 teaspoons fish sauce
1 tablespoon water
½ cup (110g) mashed potato
2 sheets ready-rolled
   frozen puff pastry
1 egg, beaten lightly
vegetable oil, for deep frying
sweet chilli dipping sauce
4 small fresh red thai chillies,
   chopped coarsely
3 cloves garlic, quartered
¾ cup (180ml) white vinegar
⅓ cup (25g) caster sugar
½ teaspoon salt
½ teaspoon tamarind paste

Make sweet chilli dipping sauce.
Heat oil in wok or large frying pan; stir-fry coriander root, onion, garlic and beef until beef is changed in colour. Add spices; stir-fry until fragrant. Add fish sauce and the water; simmer, uncovered, until mixture thickens. Stir in potato; cool.
Using 9cm cutter, cut four rounds from each pastry sheet. Place 1 level tablespoon of the filling in centre of each round; brush around edge lightly with egg. Fold pastry over to enclose filling, pressing edges together to seal.
Just before serving, heat oil in large saucepan; deep-fry curry puffs, in batches, until crisp and browned lightly. Drain on absorbent paper; serve with dipping sauce.
Sweet chilli dipping sauce Combine ingredients in small saucepan, stir over heat without boiling until sugar is dissolved; bring to a boil. Reduce heat; simmer, uncovered, about 10 minutes or until slightly thickened. Cool 5 minutes; blend or process until pureed.

makes 8
per curry puff 8.3g fat; 538kJ (129 cal)
do ahead Uncooked curry puffs can be made a day ahead; store, covered, in the refrigerator. Sweet chilli dipping sauce can be made a week ahead; store, covered, in the refrigerator.

spicy chicken salad in witlof

1 tablespoon sesame oil
300g chicken mince
1 tablespoon fish sauce
2 tablespoons lime juice
1 tablespoon grated palm sugar
1 tablespoon finely chopped vietnamese mint
1 tablespoon finely chopped fresh coriander
4 baby witlof, separated

paste
2 coriander roots, chopped coarsely
3 cloves garlic, peeled
2cm piece fresh ginger (10g), grated
10 white peppercorns

Heat oil in wok or large frying pan, add paste;
cook, stirring, until fragrant.
Add chicken; cook, stirring, until browned all over.
Add sauce, juice and sugar to pan; simmer gently,
uncovered, a few minutes or until thickened slightly.
Stir in mint and coriander.
Divide mixture evenly among witlof leaves.
Paste In small blender, spice grinder, or mortar and
pestle, blend or pound ingredients together until
finely chopped.

makes 24
per leaf 1.8g fat; 121kJ (29 cal)
do ahead The chicken filling can be prepared
several hours ahead; reheat filling and assemble
close to serving time.

potato skins

5 medium potatoes (1kg), unpeeled
2 tablespoons olive oil
½ cup (120g) sour cream

Preheat oven to hot.
Scrub potatoes well; brush with half of the oil.
Place potatoes on oven tray; bake, uncovered,
in hot oven about 50 minutes or until tender. Cool.
Cut each potato into six wedges; carefully remove
flesh, leaving skins intact. Place potato skins,
skin-side down, on wire rack over oven tray;
brush with remaining oil. Roast, uncovered,
in hot oven about 20 minutes or until crisp;
serve with sour cream.

makes 30
per potato skin 1.2g fat; 99kJ (24 cal)
per tablespoon sour cream 7.9g fat; 312kJ (75 cal)
do ahead The potatoes can be prepared several
hours ahead; cook skins just before serving.

prawn wontons
with sweet chilli sauce

1kg uncooked medium
   prawns
3 green onions,
   chopped coarsely
4cm piece fresh
   ginger (20g), grated
1 clove garlic, quartered
1 tablespoon lime juice
1 tablespoon finely chopped
   fresh vietnamese mint
1 tablespoon finely chopped
   fresh thai basil
40 wonton wrappers
1 egg, beaten lightly
½ cup (125ml) sweet
   chilli sauce

Shell and devein prawns.

Blend or process prawns, onion, ginger, garlic and juice until mixture forms a paste. Stir in mint and basil.

Place 1 heaped teaspoon of prawn filling in centre of each wonton wrapper. Brush edges with egg; pinch edges together to seal.

Place wontons, in batches, in single layer in bamboo steamer. Cook, covered, over wok or large saucepan of simmering water about 10 minutes or until wontons are cooked through.

Serve wontons with sweet chilli sauce.

makes 40

per wonton 0.3g fat; 131kJ (31 cal)

tip You can deep-fry wontons in vegetable oil, in batches, until browned all over.

do ahead Uncooked wontons are suitable to freeze; use a sheet of baking paper between each layer of wontons. There's no need to defrost them before cooking.

serving suggestion Serve steamed wontons either using the bamboo steamer as a tray or sit each wonton on a porcelain Chinese soup spoon, drizzle with sweet chilli sauce then pass around on trays to guests.

mixed satay sticks

250g chicken breast fillet
250g beef eye fillet
250g pork fillet
2 cloves garlic, crushed
2 teaspoons brown sugar
¼ teaspoon sambal oelek
1 teaspoon ground turmeric
¼ teaspoon curry powder
½ teaspoon ground cumin
½ teaspoon ground
    coriander
2 tablespoons peanut oil

satay sauce

½ cup (80g) roasted
    unsalted peanuts
2 tablespoons
    red curry paste
¾ cup (180ml) coconut milk
¼ cup (60ml) chicken stock
1 tablespoon kaffir lime juice
1 tablespoon brown sugar

Cut chicken, beef and pork into long 1.5cm-thick strips; thread strips onto skewers. Place skewers, in single layer, on oven tray or in shallow baking dish; brush with combined garlic, sugar, sambal, spices and oil. Cover; refrigerate 3 hours or overnight.

Meanwhile, make satay sauce.

Cook skewers on heated oiled grill plate (or grill or barbecue) until browned all over and cooked as desired. Serve immediately with satay sauce.

Satay sauce Blend or process nuts until chopped finely; add curry paste, process until just combined. Bring coconut milk to a boil in small saucepan; add peanut mixture, whisking until smooth. Reduce heat, add stock; cook, stirring, about 3 minutes or until sauce thickens slightly. Add juice and sugar, stirring, until sugar dissolves.

makes 12 skewers

per skewer 13.2g fat; 406kJ (97 cal)

do ahead The skewers and sauce can be prepared a day ahead; store, covered, in the refrigerator. Cook the skewers just before serving.

caramelised garlic and blue cheese tartlets

20g butter
1 tablespoon olive oil
12 cloves garlic, peeled, halved lengthways
1 large leek (500g), sliced thinly
2 teaspoons brown sugar
1 sheet ready-rolled puff pastry
60g blue cheese, crumbled

Preheat oven to hot.
Heat butter and oil in large frying pan; cook garlic, stirring, over very low heat about 10 minutes or until soft and browned lightly. Remove from pan.
Add leek to same pan; cook, stirring, until soft. Add sugar; cook, stirring occasionally, about 15 minutes or until mixture caramelises.
Cut rounds from pastry sheet using 4.5cm cutter. Place rounds on greased oven tray and put another greased oven tray on top (this cooks pastry through, but prevents it from rising).
Bake rounds in hot oven about 10 minutes or until browned lightly. Remove top oven tray.
Divide cheese among pastry rounds; top with caramelised leek and pieces of garlic. Return tartlets to oven for about 2 minutes or until cheese is soft.

makes 24
per tartlet 3.9g fat; 222kJ (53 cal)
do ahead The pastry rounds can be made a day ahead; the garlic and leek mixture can be made up to eight hours ahead. Top pastry rounds and reheat just before serving.

lamb kofta with spiced yogurt

¼ cup (40g) burghul

500g lamb mince

1 egg

1 medium brown onion
(150g), chopped finely

¼ cup (40g) pine nuts,
chopped finely

2 tablespoons finely
chopped fresh mint

2 tablespoons finely
chopped fresh
flat-leaf parsley

vegetable oil,
for shallow-frying

spiced yogurt

1 small fresh red thai chilli,
seeded, chopped finely

1 tablespoon finely chopped
fresh mint

1 tablespoon finely chopped
fresh flat-leaf parsley

1 tablespoon finely chopped
fresh coriander

1 clove garlic, crushed

½ teaspoon ground cumin

¾ cup (200g) thick yogurt

Cover burghul with cold water in small bowl; stand 10 minutes. Drain; pat dry with absorbent paper to remove as much water as possible.

Using hands, combine burghul in large bowl with lamb, egg, onion, nuts and herbs. Roll rounded teaspoons of the lamb mixture into kofta balls. Place on tray, cover; refrigerate 30 minutes.

Meanwhile, make spiced yogurt.

Heat oil in large frying pan; shallow-fry kofta, in batches, until browned all over and cooked through. Drain on absorbent paper. Serve hot with spiced yogurt.

Spiced yogurt Combine ingredients in medium bowl.

makes 40 kofta and ¾ cup spiced yogurt

per kofta 3.8g fat; 205kJ (49 cal)

per tablespoon spiced yogurt
0.8g fat; 71kJ (17 cal)

do ahead The uncooked kofta and spiced yogurt can be made a day ahead; store separately, covered, in the refrigerator.

kumara and pea samosas with cucumber yogurt

Samosas are deep-fried Indian pastries filled with vegetables or meat, or a combination of both.

1 medium potato (200g), chopped coarsely
1 medium kumara (400g), chopped coarsely
1 cup (125g) frozen peas
20g ghee
1 medium brown onion (150g), chopped finely
1 clove garlic, crushed
2cm piece fresh ginger (10g), grated
1 teaspoon ground cumin
½ teaspoon ground coriander
¼ teaspoon garam masala
6 sheets ready-rolled puff pastry
vegetable oil, for deep-frying
cucumber yogurt
1 lebanese cucumber (130g), seeded, chopped coarsely
1 tablespoon chopped fresh mint
¾ cup (200g) yogurt
1 clove garlic, quartered
1 tablespoon lemon juice

Boil, steam or microwave potato, kumara and peas, separately, until tender; drain.
Meanwhile, heat ghee in medium frying pan; cook onion, garlic and ginger, stirring, until onion is soft. Add spices; cook, stirring, until fragrant.
Mash potato and kumara together in large bowl until almost smooth. Add peas and onion mixture; stir to combine.
Using a 7.5cm cutter, cut nine rounds from each pastry sheet. Place 1 heaped teaspoon of filling in centre of each round; pinch edges together to seal.
Make cucumber yogurt.
Heat oil in wok or large saucepan; deep-fry samosas, in batches, until browned all over. Drain on absorbent paper; serve with cucumber yogurt.
Cucumber yogurt Blend or process ingredients until combined.

makes 54 samosas and ¾ cup cucumber yogurt
per samosa 2.6g fat; 173kJ (41 cal)
per tablespoon cucumber yogurt 0.5g fat; 73kJ (17 cal)

tip As an alternative to deep-frying, bake samosas, uncovered, in a moderate oven about 30 minutes or until browned.

do ahead Uncooked samosas are suitable to freeze; use a sheet of baking paper between each layer of samosas. There's no need to defrost them before cooking.

gyoza with soy vinegar sauce

300g pork mince

2 tablespoons kecap manis

1 teaspoon sugar

1 tablespoon sake

1 egg, beaten lightly

2 teaspoons sesame oil

3 cups (240g) finely
shredded chinese
cabbage

4 green onions, sliced thinly

40 gyoza or gow gee
wrappers

1 tablespoon vegetable oil

soy vinegar sauce

½ cup (125ml) light
soy sauce

¼ cup (60ml) red
wine vinegar

2 tablespoons white vinegar

2 tablespoons sweet
chilli sauce

Combine pork, kecap manis, sugar, sake, egg, sesame oil, cabbage and onion in large bowl; refrigerate 1 hour.

Meanwhile make soy vinegar sauce.

Place one heaped teaspoon of the pork mixture in centre of one wrapper; brush one edge of wrapper with a little water. Pleat damp side of wrapper only; pinch both sides together to seal. Repeat with remaining pork mixture and wrappers.

Cover base of large frying pan with water; bring to a boil. Add dumplings, in batches; reduce heat, simmer, covered, 3 minutes. Using slotted spoon, remove dumplings from pan. Drain pan; dry thoroughly.

Heat vegetable oil in same pan; cook dumplings, in batches, unpleated side and base only, until golden brown. Serve hot with soy vinegar sauce.

Soy vinegar sauce Combine ingredients in small bowl.

makes 40

per gyoza 1.4g fat; 150kJ (36 cal)

do ahead Gyoza filling can be prepared up to 4 hours ahead; store, covered, in the refrigerator. Soy vinegar sauce can be made a day ahead; store, covered, in the refrigerator.

risotto-filled zucchini flowers

1 cup (250ml) dry white wine
2 cups (500ml)
   vegetable stock
½ cup (125ml) water
1 tablespoon olive oil
1 small brown onion (80g),
   chopped finely
1 clove garlic, crushed
1 cup (200g) arborio rice
150g button mushrooms,
   sliced thinly
2 trimmed silverbeet leaves
   (160g), chopped finely
¼ cup (20g) finely grated
   parmesan cheese
48 tiny zucchini with
   flowers attached
cooking-oil spray

Combine wine, stock and the water in large saucepan; bring to a boil. Reduce heat; simmer, covered, to keep hot.

Meanwhile, heat oil in large saucepan; cook onion and garlic, stirring, until onion softens. Add rice; stir to coat in onion mixture. Stir in 1 cup of the hot stock mixture; cook, stirring, over low heat until liquid is absorbed. Continue adding hot stock mixture, in 1-cup batches, stirring, until liquid is absorbed after each addition. Total cooking time should be about 35 minutes or until rice is tender.

Add mushrooms and silverbeet; cook, stirring, until mushrooms are just tender. Stir in cheese.

Remove and discard stamens from centre of flowers; fill flowers with risotto, twist petal tops to enclose filling.

Cook zucchini with flowers, in batches, on heated oiled grill plate (or grill or barbecue) until zucchini are just tender and risotto is heated through.

makes 48
per flower 0.7g fat; 121kJ (29 cal)
do ahead The risotto can be prepared a day ahead. Spread risotto on tray, cover; refrigerate until required.

beetroot dip

3 medium trimmed beetroot (500g)
1 clove garlic, crushed
¾ cup (200g) yogurt
1 teaspoon ground cumin
2 teaspoons lemon juice

Cook unpeeled beetroot in large saucepan of
boiling water, uncovered, about 45 minutes or
until tender. Drain; cool 5 minutes. Wearing gloves,
peel beetroot while warm; chop coarsely.
Blend or process beetroot with garlic, yogurt,
cumin and juice until smooth.

makes 2 cups (585g)
per tablespoon 0.3g fat; 63kJ (15 cal)
do ahead This dip can be made up to two days
ahead; store, covered, in the refrigerator.
serving suggestion Serve with crackers, crudités
or toasted shards of pitta.

rosti with smoked salmon

800g potatoes, peeled
15g butter, melted
1 tablespoon finely chopped fresh dill
½ cup (125ml) olive oil
200g crème fraîche
200g smoked salmon, sliced
dill for garnish, extra

Coarsely grate potatoes, squeeze out excess liquid. In medium bowl, combine potato, butter and dill.

Heat a little of the olive oil in large non-stick frying pan. Place an oiled 5cm-round metal cutter in pan and fill with 1 tablespoon of the potato mixture, pressing with back of spoon to flatten. Remove the cutter carefully (it will be hot) and repeat with remaining potato mixture and olive oil. Cook rosti until golden on each side; drain on absorbent paper, cool.

Place 1 teaspoon of crème fraîche on each rosti to serve; top with salmon and extra dill.

makes 24
per rosti 7.3g fat; 392kJ (94 cal)
do ahead The rosti can be made several hours ahead; assemble close to serving time.

fetta dip

200g fetta cheese, crumbled
¾ cup (150g) ricotta cheese
2 tablespoons lemon juice
2 tablespoons olive oil
1 clove garlic, quartered

Process ingredients until smooth.

makes 1¾ cups (385g)
per tablespoon 4.8g fat; 225kJ (59 cal)
do ahead This recipe can be made up
to two days ahead; store, covered,
in the refrigerator.
serving suggestion Serve with crackers,
crudités or toasted shards of pitta.

mini zucchini frittatas

You need four 12-hole non-stick mini
(1½ tablespoons/30ml) muffin pans for this recipe.
If you do not own that many, make the frittatas in
batches, placing the cooked ones on a wire rack
while you make the remainder.

8 eggs
1 cup (240g) sour cream
¼ cup finely chopped fresh chives
1 large yellow zucchini (150g), grated coarsely
1 large green zucchini (150g), grated coarsely
⅓ cup (25g) finely grated parmesan cheese
2 tablespoons coarsely chopped fresh chives, extra

Preheat oven to moderate. Lightly oil four
12-hole mini muffin pans.
Whisk eggs with two-thirds of the sour cream
in large bowl until smooth; stir in chives, zucchini
and cheese.
Divide mixture among holes of prepared pans.
Bake, uncovered, in moderate oven 15 minutes;
turn onto wire rack to cool.
Top frittatas with remaining sour cream and
extra chives.
Serve at room temperature.

makes 48
per frittata 3.1g fat; 142kJ (34 cal)
do ahead Frittatas can be made a day ahead
and stored, covered, in the refrigerator.

cheese balls with four coatings

Neufchâtel cheese is similar in flavour and appearance to cream cheese. Farm cheese comes in a variety of tastes and textures, from mild and sliceable to dry and crumbly.

500g neufchâtel cheese
500g farm cheese
2 teaspoons finely grated
   lemon rind
2 tablespoons lemon juice
¼ teaspoon sea salt

Line four oven trays with baking paper. Blend or process ingredients until smooth; refrigerate about 2 hours or until firm enough to roll. Using hands, roll rounded teaspoons of the mixture into balls; place 16 balls on each of prepared trays. Refrigerate, covered, until firm. Roll 16 balls in each of the four coatings. Serve cold.

makes 64

pepper coating
Coat balls in a mixture of 1½ tablespoons poppy seeds and 2 teaspoons cracked black pepper.

per ball 4.5g fat; 217kJ (52 cal)

za'atar coating
Combine 1 tablespoon each of sumac and toasted sesame seeds, 1 teaspoon each of dried oregano, dried marjoram and sweet paprika, and 2 teaspoons dried thyme; coat balls in mix.

per ball 4.5g fat; 217kJ (52 cal)

sesame seed coating
Coat balls in ¼ cup (35g) sesame seeds.

per ball 4.7g fat; 224kJ (53 cal)

parsley coating
Coat balls in ½ cup finely chopped fresh flat-leaf parsley.

per ball 4.4g fat; 210kJ (50 cal)

vietnamese rice paper rolls

1 tablespoon peanut oil

2 chicken breast fillets (340g)

12 x 17cm-square rice
    paper sheets

1 small red capsicum (150g),
    sliced thinly

1¼ cups (100g) bean sprouts

½ cup firmly packed
    fresh mint leaves

½ cup firmly packed fresh
    coriander leaves

dipping sauce

1 clove garlic, crushed

2 tablespoons fish sauce

¼ cup (60ml) lime juice

¼ cup (60ml) oyster sauce

¼ cup (65g) finely grated
    palm sugar

2 small fresh red thai chillies,
    seeded, chopped finely

Heat oil in small frying pan; cook chicken until browned all over and cooked through. Stand 10 minutes; slice thinly into 24 pieces.

Meanwhile, make dipping sauce.

Place one sheet of rice paper in medium bowl of warm water until just softened; carefully lift from water. Place on board; pat dry with absorbent paper. Position rice paper in diamond shape; place two chicken slices vertically down centre of rice paper, top with capsicum, sprouts, mint and coriander. Fold bottom corner over filling; roll rice paper from side to side to enclose filling. Repeat with remaining rice paper sheets and filling.

Serve cold rice paper rolls with dipping sauce.

Dipping sauce Combine ingredients in small saucepan; stir over medium heat until sugar dissolves. Refrigerate until cold.

makes 12

per roll 3.4g fat; 730kJ (174 cal)

do ahead The chicken can be cooked and the dipping sauce made a day ahead; store separately, covered, in the refrigerator. Assemble just before serving time.

prosciutto-wrapped bocconcini

7 very thin slices (85g) prosciutto
50 small basil leaves
50 drained cherry bocconcini (600g)
freshly ground black pepper, optional, for serving
caperberries, optional, for serving

Cut prosciutto in half widthways. Cut each
half into four strips lengthways.
Hold a basil leaf against one ball of bocconcini
and wrap a strip of prosciutto around the leaf
and cheese. Repeat with remaining basil leaves,
bocconcini and prosciutto.
Grind a little black pepper over bocconcini and
serve on a platter with caperberries, if desired.

makes 50
per bocconcini 0.1g fat; 27kJ (6 cal)
do ahead This recipe can be made three hours
ahead; store, covered, in the refrigerator.

peking duck wraps

8 green onions, trimmed
¼ cup (60ml) hoisin sauce
1 tablespoon plum sauce
2 cups (250g) thinly sliced chinese
    barbecued duck meat
16 small butter lettuce leaves

Cut white sections from green onions; reserve. Dip green sections in medium heatproof bowl of boiling water for 5 seconds, then place in medium bowl of cold water; drain. Thinly slice reserved white sections.

Divide combined sauces, duck and slices of white section of onion among lettuce leaves. Roll lettuce to enclose filling; tie each wrap with one piece of green section of onion to secure.

Serve wraps cold or at room temperature.

makes 16
per wrap 4.3g fat; 560kJ (62 cal)
tip You may need extra green onions to ensure you have enough green sections to wrap the lettuce leaves.

do ahead Buy a whole large barbecued duck from a Chinese food shop the day before serving this recipe. Remove and discard skin and bones; slice the meat thinly. Store meat, covered, in the refrigerator.

goat cheese and garlic bruschetta

Ciabatta is crusty Italian bread.

1 loaf ciabatta
¼ cup (60ml) olive oil
2 cloves garlic, crushed
300g goat cheese
¼ small red onion (25g), sliced thinly
2 tablespoons olive oil, extra
freshly ground black pepper
50g baby rocket leaves

Cut bread into 16 x 1cm-thick slices. Brush
one side of bread with combined oil and garlic.
Grill bread until browned lightly on both sides.
Using a hot, wet knife, slice cheese thinly. Divide
cheese evenly among toasted bread. (If cheese is
too soft to slice, spread on toast instead.)
Top bruschetta with onion, extra olive oil, black
pepper and rocket leaves.

makes 16
per bruschetta 8.9g fat; 711kJ (170 cal)
do ahead This recipe is best made close to
serving time.

glossary

arborio rice small, round-grain rice well suited to absorb large amount of liquid; especially suitable for risottos.

bean sprouts also known as bean shoots; tender new growths of assorted beans and seeds germinated for consumption as sprouts.

beetroot also known as red beets; round root vegetable.

besan flour made from ground chickpeas. Also known as gram or besan flour.

bicarbonate of soda also known as baking soda.

breadcrumbs
packaged dry: fine-textured, crunchy, purchased, white breadcrumbs.
stale: one- or two-day-old bread made into crumbs by blending or processing.

burghul also called bulghur wheat; hulled steamed wheat kernels crushed, once dried, into grains.

caperberries fruit formed after the caper buds have flowered; caperberries are pickled, usually with stalks intact.

capsicum also known as bell pepper or, simply, pepper. Are red, green, yellow, orange or purplish black. Discard seeds and membranes before use.

chilli available in many types and sizes. Use rubber gloves when seeding and chopping fresh chillies as they can burn your skin. Remove seeds and membrane to reduce the heat.
flakes: deep-red, dried, fine slices and whole seeds.
powder: the Asian variety is the hottest, made from dried ground thai chillies; use as a substitute for fresh chillies in

proportion of ½ teaspoon ground chilli powder to 1 medium chopped fresh chilli.
small fresh thai: bright red in colour; small and medium-hot.
sweet sauce: thin Thai sauce made from red chillies, sugar, garlic and vinegar.

chinese cabbage also known as peking or napa cabbage, wong bok or petsai. Elongated with pale green, crinkly leaves.

ciabatta meaning slipper in Italian; the traditional shape of this crisp-crusted white bread.

coconut milk not the juice found inside the fruit (coconut water), but the diluted liquid from the second pressing of the white meat of a mature coconut (the first pressing produces coconut cream). Available in cans and cartons at supermarkets.

coriander also known as pak chee, cilantro or chinese parsley; bright-green leafy herb with a pungent flavour.

cornflour also known as cornstarch; used as a thickening agent in cooking.

crème fraîche (minimum fat content 35%) mature fermented cream having a slightly tangy, nutty flavour and velvety texture.

eggs some recipes in this book call for raw or barely cooked eggs; exercise caution if there is a salmonella problem in your area.

fillo pastry also called phyllo; tissue-thin pastry sheets purchased chilled or frozen.

fish sauce also called nam pla or nuoc nam. Made from pulverised, salted, fermented fish (most often anchovies);

has a pungent smell and strong taste. There are many versions of varying intensity, so use according to taste.

flour, plain an all-purpose flour, made from wheat.

garam masala a blend of spices, originating in North India; based on proportions of cardamom, cinnamon, cloves, coriander, fennel and cumin, roasted and ground together. Black pepper and chilli can be added for a hotter version.

ghee clarified butter; with the milk solids removed, this fat can be heated to a high temperature without burning.

ginger also known as green or root ginger; the thick gnarled root of a tropical plant.

gow gee wrappers also known as gow gee pastry. Spring roll or egg pastry sheets or wonton wrappers can be substituted.

hoisin sauce a thick, sweet and spicy Chinese paste made from salted fermented soy beans, onions and garlic.

kaffir lime leaves leaves from a small citrus tree.

kecap manis also known as sieu wan; a dark, thick, sweet soy sauce used in most South-East Asian cuisines. Depending on the brand, the soy's sweetness is derived from the addition of molasses or palm sugar when brewed.

kumara Polynesian name of orange-fleshed sweet potato often confused with yam.

lemon grass a tall, clumping, lemon-smelling and -tasting, sharp-edged grass; the white lower part of the stem is used, finely chopped, in cooking.

mince meat also known as ground meat, as in beef, pork, chicken, lamb and veal.

oil

cooking-oil spray: we use a cholesterol-free cooking spray made from canola oil.

olive: made from ripened olives. Extra virgin and virgin are the first and second pressings, respectively, and are thought the best; extra light or light is diluted and refers to taste not fat levels.

peanut: pressed from ground peanuts; most commonly used oil in Asian cooking because of its high smoke point (capacity to handle high heat without burning).

sesame: made from roasted, crushed, white sesame seeds; a flavouring rather than a cooking medium.

vegetable: oil sourced from plants rather than animal fats.

onion

green: also known as scallion or (incorrectly) shallot; an immature onion picked before the bulb has formed, having a long, bright-green edible stalk.

red: also known as spanish, red spanish or bermuda onion; a sweet-flavoured, large, purple-red onion.

oyster sauce a rich, brown sauce made from oysters and their brine, cooked with salt and soy sauce, and thickened with starches.

parsley, flat-leaf also called continental or italian parsley.

ready-rolled pastry packaged sheets of frozen pastry, found in supermarkets.

pine nuts also known as pignoli; not actually a nut, but a small, cream-coloured kernel from pine cones.

plum sauce a thick, sweet and sour dipping sauce made from plums, vinegar, sugar, chillies and spices.

prawns also called shrimp.

prosciutto salt-cured, air-dried (unsmoked) pressed ham; usually sold in paper-thin slices, ready to eat.

rice paper sheets also called banh trang. Made from rice paste and stamped into rounds; store well at room temperature. They're brittle and will break if dropped; dip momentarily in water for pliable wrappers.

rocket also called arugula, rugula and rucola; a peppery-tasting green leaf. Baby rocket leaves are both smaller and less peppery.

sake Japan's favourite rice wine. If sake is unavailable, use dry sherry instead.

sambal oelek also ulek or olek; Indonesian in origin; a salty paste made from ground chillies and vinegar.

sesame seeds black and white are the most common of this small oval seed, but they are also red and brown. A good source of calcium. To toast: spread seeds evenly on oven tray, toast in moderate oven briefly.

silverbeet also called swiss chard or chard; a leafy, dark green vegetable, related to the beet, with thick, crisp white or red stems and ribs. Leaves, often trimmed from stems and ribs, are used raw or cooked.

spring roll wrappers also called egg roll wrappers; they come in various sizes, fresh or frozen, from Asian food stores. Made from a delicate wheat-based pastry, can be used for making gow gee, samosas and spring rolls.

sugar

caster: also known as superfine sugar.

palm: made from the sap of the sugar palm tree. Light-brown to black in colour and sold in rock-hard cakes; use brown sugar if unavailable.

tamarind paste also called tamarind concentrate. Is made when tamarind juice is distilled into a condensed, compacted paste. Thick and purple-black, is ready-to-use, no soaking or straining required; dilute with water according to taste. Adds zing to sauces, curries, chutneys and marinades.

turmeric also called kamin; a rhizome related to galangal and ginger, must be grated or pounded to release its acrid aroma and pungent flavour. Known for the golden colour it imparts to other ingredients. Fresh turmeric can be substituted with dried powder (use 2 teaspoons ground turmeric plus 1 teaspoon sugar for every 20g fresh turmeric called for in a recipe).

witlof also known as chicory or belgian endive.

wonton wrappers made of flour, eggs, and water, they come in varying thicknesses. Sold in the refrigerated section of Asian grocery stores; gow gee, egg or spring roll pastry sheets can be substituted.

zucchini also known as courgette.

conversion chart

MEASURES

One Australian metric measuring cup holds approximately 250ml, one Australian metric tablespoon holds 20ml, one Australian metric teaspoon holds 5ml.

The difference between one country's measuring cups and another's is within a 2- or 3-teaspoon variance, and will not affect your cooking results. North America, New Zealand and the United Kingdom use a 15ml tablespoon. All cup and spoon measurements are level. The most accurate way of measuring dry ingredients is to weigh them. When measuring liquids, use a clear glass or plastic jug with metric markings.

We use large eggs with an average weight of 60g.

DRY MEASURES

METRIC	IMPERIAL
15g	½oz
30g	1oz
60g	2oz
90g	3oz
125g	4oz (¼lb)
155g	5oz
185g	6oz
220g	7oz
250g	8oz (½lb)
280g	9oz
315g	10oz
345g	11oz
375g	12oz (¾lb)
410g	13oz
440g	14oz
470g	15oz
500g	16oz (1lb)
750g	24oz (1½lb)
1kg	32oz (2lb)

LIQUID MEASURES

METRIC	IMPERIAL
30ml	1 fluid oz
60ml	2 fluid oz
100ml	3 fluid oz
125ml	4 fluid oz
150ml	5 fluid oz (¼ pint/1 gill)
190ml	6 fluid oz
250ml	8 fluid oz
300ml	10 fluid oz (½ pint)
500ml	16 fluid oz
600ml	20 fluid oz (1 pint)
1000ml (1 litre)	1¾ pints

LENGTH MEASURES

METRIC	IMPERIAL
3mm	⅛in
6mm	¼in
1cm	½in
2cm	¾in
2.5cm	1in
5cm	2in
6cm	2½in
8cm	3in
10cm	4in
13cm	5in
15cm	6in
18cm	7in
20cm	8in
23cm	9in
25cm	10in
28cm	11in
30cm	12in (1ft)

OVEN TEMPERATURES

These oven temperatures are only a guide for conventional ovens. For fan-forced ovens, check the manufacturer's manual.

	°C (CELSIUS)	°F (FAHRENHEIT)	GAS MARK
Very slow	120	250	½
Slow	150	275 – 300	1 – 2
Moderately slow	160	325	3
Moderate	180	350 – 375	4 – 5
Moderately hot	200	400	6
Hot	220	425 – 450	7 – 8
Very hot	240	475	9

index

Are you missing some of the world's favourite cookbooks?

The Australian Women's Weekly cookbooks are available from bookshops, cookshops, supermarkets and other stores all over the world. You can also buy direct from the publisher, using the order form below.

MINI SERIES £3.50 190x138MM 64 PAGES

TITLE	QTY	TITLE	QTY	TITLE	QTY
4 Fast Ingredients		Dried Fruit & Nuts		Party Food	
15-minute Feasts		Drinks		Pasta	
30-minute Meals		Fast Food for Friends		Pickles and Chutneys	
50 Fast Chicken Fillets		Fast Soup		Potatoes	
50 Fast Desserts (Oct 06)		Finger Food		Risotto	
After-work Stir-fries		Gluten-free Cooking		Roast	
Barbecue		Healthy Everyday Food 4 Kids		Salads	
Barbecue Chicken		Ice-creams & Sorbets		Simple Slices	
Barbecued Seafood		Indian Cooking		Simply Seafood	
Biscuits, Brownies & Biscotti		Indonesian Favourites		Skinny Food	
Bites		Italian		Spanish Favourites	
Bowl Food		Italian Favourites		Stir-fries	
Burgers, Rösti & Fritters		Jams & Jellies		Summer Salads	
Cafe Cakes		Japanese Favourites		Tapas, Antipasto & Mezze	
Cafe Food		Kids Party Food		Thai Cooking	
Casseroles		Last-minute Meals		Thai Favourites	
Char-grills & Barbecues		Lebanese Cooking		The Fast Egg	
Cheesecakes, Pavlova & Trifles		Low Fat Fast		The Packed Lunch	
Chinese Favourites		Malaysian Favourites		Vegetarian	
Chocolate Cakes		Mince		Vegetarian Stir-fries	
Christmas Cakes & Puddings		Mince Favourites		Vegie Main Meals	
Cocktails		Muffins		Wok	
Crumbles & Bakes		Noodles		Young Chef	
Curries		Outdoor Eating		TOTAL COST £	

Photocopy and complete coupon below

Name _____

Address _____

_____ Postcode _____

Country _____ Phone (business hours) _____

Email*(optional) _____
* By including your email address, you consent to receipt of any email regarding this magazine, and other emails which inform you of ACP's other publications, products, services and events, and to promote third party goods and services you may be interested in.

I enclose my cheque/money order for £ _____ or please charge £ _____
to my: ☐ Access ☐ Mastercard ☐ Visa ☐ Diners Club
PLEASE NOTE: WE DO NOT ACCEPT SWITCH OR ELECTRON CARDS

Card number | | | | | | | | | | | | | | | |

3 digit security code *(found on reverse of card)* _____

Cardholder's
signature _____ Expiry date ____ / ____

To order: Mail or fax – photocopy or complete the order form above, and send your credit card details or cheque payable to: Australian Consolidated Press (UK), Moulton Park Business Centre, Red House Road, Moulton Park, Northampton NN3 6AQ, phone (+44) (01) 604 497531, fax (+44) (01) 604 497533, e-mail books@acpmedia.co.uk. Or order online at www.acpuk.com
Non-UK residents: We accept the credit cards listed on the coupon, or cheques, drafts or International Money Orders payable in sterling and drawn on a UK bank. Credit card charges are at the exchange rate current at the time of payment.
All pricing current at time of going to press and subject to change/availability.
Postage and packing UK: Add £1.00 per order plus 25p per book.
Postage and packing overseas: Add £2.00 per order plus 50p per book. **Offer ends 31.12.2007**